SOMEWHERE OTHER

John Wardle
Architects

SOMEWHERE
OTHER

Uro
Publications

Either transportable pavilion or unrealized idea, Camillo's model was intended to exist as an *actual* miniature theater, only large enough for one spectator-scholar, who would stand in the center, the stage-area. The "spectator" would use the device to learn the structure of the universe in an encyclopedic ritual.

—From Dan Graham,
Theatre, Cinema, Power

We cross from one reality...
    to another reality.
From one street...
    to another street.
From one setting...
    to another setting.

—From John Berendt,
The City of Falling Angels

CONTENTS

8

SOMEWHERE	John
OTHER	Wardle
MAKING	
SOMEWHERE	Jacaranda Industries
OTHER	&
PICTURING	Tensys
SOMEWHERE	&
OTHER	Derek John
PICTURING	
SOMEWHERE	Photographed
OTHER	by
WORKS	Trevor Mein
MAKE	
FRIENDS	John Wardle
ILLUSIONS	Architects
& ALLUSIONS	&
A FRACTURED	Friends
IMAGE	
ON MAKING	Natasha
OBJECTS	Johns-
OTHER	Messenger
PORTALS	
APERTURES,	Coco
PORTALS &	&
THE FRAMING	Maximilian
OF SOMEWHERE	
OTHER	Australian Tapestry Workshop

SOMEWHERE
OTHER
MAKING
SOMEWHERE
OTHER
PICTURING
SOMEWHERE
OTHER
WORKS
MAKE
FRIENDS
ILLUSIONS
& ALLUSIONS
A FRACTURED
IMAGE
ON MAKING
OBJECTS
OTHER
PORTALS
APERTURES,
PORTALS &
THE FRAMING
OF SOMEWHERE
OTHER

John
Wardle

Jacaranda Industries
&
Tensys
&
Derek John

Photographed
by
Trevor Mein

John Wardle
Architects
&
Friends

Natasha
Johns-
Messenger

Coco
&
Maximilian

Australian Tapestry Workshop
&
Leonardo Cimolin

Rory
Hyde

Max
Delany

John
Wardle

SOMEWHERE OTHER

Palladio's Teatro
Olimpico, in
Vincenza.

In August 2017 an email arrived from Yvonne Farrell and Shelley
McNamara inviting us to participate in the 2018 Venice Biennale.
Their invitation requested that we submit a proposal that would align
our processes and explorations with the biennale theme, as outlined
in their remarkable manifesto *Freespace*.

Drawing upon a pool of people and ideas within the practice,
we considered many possibilities over two working sessions. An idea
emerged from the discussion, formed around the theme of translation
and working between two distinctly different places. This genesis
borrowed from a link already made between our practice and Venice.

In 2015 we were joint winners of the inaugural Tapestry Design
Prize for Architects. Our tapestry design, later to be commissioned by
the Australian philanthropist Judith Neilson and produced by the
Australian Tapestry Workshop, refers to an exchange between Australia
and Italy. The competition brief suggested that the tapestry would be
hung within the then newly completed Australian Pavilion in the
Giardini in Venice. This space is a quintessential white cube: a neutral
volume that is intentionally mute, with no pronounced proportional bias.

A counterpoint to this pavilion is Palladio's Teatro Olimpico
in Vicenza, with its fine arched portals and classical sets of streetscapes

in exaggerated diminishing perspective created by Vincenzo Scamozzi. We created an imagined space for the tapestry that reversed Scamozzi's inverted perspectives, forming a series of picture planes drawn toward the audience. Each plane multiplied shifting perspectives across one wall, while allowing another to exaggerate the proportions of the space. The partial views and variant transmissions of light within each inverted chamber suggest a place that is 'elsewhere'. This translation also referred to our own entry for the competition for the Australian Pavilion in 2012, which transferred an invented terracotta cladding system back to the Veneto, where Australian ochres would be mixed with Italian clays to create the outer face of the pavilion. Our competition entry also referred to bridges: both the actual bridges across Venetian canals and a metaphorical bridging between places, from one setting and its experiences to another. In our submission we quoted from John Berendt's *The City of Falling Angels*, when describing journeying through Venice. "We cross from one reality... to another reality. From one street... to another street. From one setting... to another setting."

Our proposal *Somewhere Other*, in response to Yvonne and Shelley, was to build the structure represented in our tapestry and take it to Venice. It was to be both bridge and portal, providing a long lens

John Wardle Architects' tapestry *Perspectives on a Flat Surface*, joint winner of the inaugural Tapestry Design Prize for Architects.

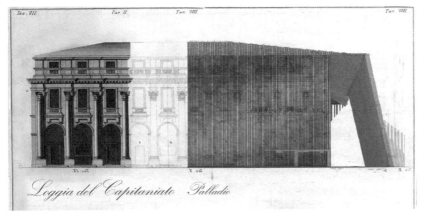

John Wardle Architects' 2012 proposal for the Australian Pavilion in Venice.

from its place with the Arsenale toward Australia. Our first iterations more directly represented the conceptual object of the tapestry. The structure was to float beneath a series of suspension members, hung from the skillion roof of the Arsenale. Soft fabric and rigid frames were to render this pavilion structure tent-like, with its spatial and temporal characteristics made possible through fabrication. Over time, these initial ideas evolved and transformed, in part through a process of creative collaboration.

For some years now, we have had a fascination with many parallel areas of creative practice, particularly in the visual arts. We have transformed many of our projects within the public realm into opportunities to engage with artists, incorporating their work into ours.

Ten years ago one such opportunity arose, when we had the rare privilege of designing a sewage museum. Our brief was to design a series of ramps and staging points within the Spotswood Victorian Pumping Station, which would allow the story to be told of the city's transformation after the creation of its sewage system in the 1880s. As part of this project the artist Natasha Johns-Messenger was commissioned to create her work *Boiler House Look-box* in the Turbine

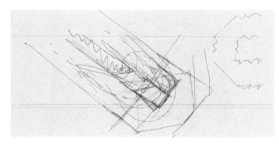

A sketch by Natasha Johns-Messenger, working out the internal mirrors.

Hall. We have maintained contact ever since, despite her move to New York, and recently commissioned a work from her, after her exhibition Sitelines at Heide Museum of Modern Art, Melbourne.

The capacity of Natasha's work to confound perception and challenge what and how we see things, led us to invite her into our project for Venice. At our very first meeting, her instruction on the metrics of composition that would enable an expanded perception of perspective, was both generous and fascinating. Importantly, she impressed upon us the accuracy and discipline that is required to trick the human mind into believing that which is not real. Natasha has schooled us in proportional geometry throughout.

For several years we have commissioned Coco and Maximilian to make short films. Now with six completed works, they have found a variety of means to express the nature of inhabitation, specific to each project. Two films, one vertical at one-to-one human scale, the other in wide format, merge places within projects, to convey the impression of a constant journey, through many portals and across many thresholds. We considered that film could provide a fine calibration to the Freespace theme. By combining the work of both of our collaborators we could extend our own narrative beyond architectural representation. The idea of expanding the potential of things, by sharing an opportunity with others, also aligns with the Freespace theme of "celebrate(ing) architecture's capacity to find additional and unexpected generosity in each project".

Our proposal went through an ungainly adolescence, as it became more of a solid structure surrounding a series of portals that would contain Natasha's mirrors and Coco and Maximilian's films. It was, by our own admission, too building-like. The decision was made to disassemble the structure from its working parts and consider it as "an instrument" – much like a camera with its casing removed to express its working functions. It was at this point that we determined our exhibition to be a series of portals and thresholds that acutely orchestrate various forms of engagement, from the most intimate to the most social, with opportunities for entering within, or standing back and observing.

While no longer the physical representation of our 'tapestry structure', this instrument for looking out beyond the confines of its place in the Arsenale employs a series of devices that play on our perception of perspective and our imagining of the space somewhere beyond.

Reviewing the steel junctions at Jacaranda Industries with Derek John.

One of a series of portals under construction.

As the project moved from sketches, drawings and discussion, to materials and fabrication it became clear that further collaboration was necessary. First, we approached Tensys, a firm of engineers who are skilled in lightweight structures. Reviewing our initial proposal, employing a tensile steel structure to support the series of extended sections, they entirely inverted the idea. They proposed a system of internal timber frames and a massive central ballast. As constructed, the fine 10mm steel rod filigree performs absolutely no structural function. Rather, it conceptually records both the iterative journey of the design process, while representing, quite literally, an architectural line drawing: defining the role of architects as proposers not makers.

Many of the stories that we tell of our buildings express the processes of their making. These narratives can incorporate conversations with those that engage us with generous ambition, to an appreciation of the vast array of skills of those employed in fabrication and construction. Our fascination with industrial processes and many forms of craft has drawn us to those that make. From this engagement, we recognise those inflections in the details of our work that reveal the hand and mind of the maker.

We invited Jacaranda Industries to join us in the project of now rapidly increasing ambition. They were the makers of the Suspended Studios in our University of Melbourne School of Design building, many interior elements of our Monash University, Learning and Teaching Building project and are about to commence on the entire interior of our Melbourne Conservatorium of Music project, which is currently under construction. They agreed without hesitation and worked late into the nights and through weekends with remarkable generosity and great skill to complete this fabrication in 21 days. These are the new craftsmen who, with digital programming, transform the Revit model generated in our office, to massive computerised CNC routers and beam saws. Our visits to their vast Geelong factory have been one of the great pleasures of our involvement with this Freespace commission.

Derek Johns has spent many years working with artists as a specialist steel fabricator. He most recently produced a large work for sculptor Simon Perry that now sits on the hill overlooking the Shearers Quarters and Captain Kelly's Cottage at Waterview, on Bruny Island, Tasmania. Working from a large industrial shed in rural Victoria, and within Jacaranda's factory, Derek has fabricated the fine steel 'script' that surrounds the entire Biennale structure, as well as the support for a fifth portal, which was a late addition to our project.

The 'Venetian Portal' suggests further linkage to the Freespace theme of expanded engagement and extends the reach of the project from Melbourne to Venice. It also suggests linkage to the portals of the tapestry that extend to *Somewhere Other* and the transference of skills mooted in our Venice Pavilion Competition.

A polished chrome cone is embedded within the wall of the passageway and concentrates a pinpointed view outwards. This view line is received by a large blown glass funnel to be made by Leonardo

Cimolin and arranged on our behalf by Francesca Giubilei of the Venice Art Factory. The view through these paired portals is then deflected by a small mirror, to extend the view back into the exhibition. This fifth portal provides a particularly resonant moment to consider the idea of translation and displacement: conceived in Australia, crafted by a specialist glass master on Murano, and supported on a framework of steel fabricated in a shed in rural Australia.

DH Lawrence wrote the novel *Kangaroo* while living in Australia in the 1920s. Writing home to England he would sign his name: "DH Lawrence – upside down at the bottom of the world". This fragment of knowledge has fascinated us for many years and has underscored a number of our projects. As Australians, we find ourselves adhered by gravity to the base of this vast hemisphere. Much of our history is that of a cultivar, drawing from the top of the world, and through adaption making it our own.

The final element in this vast composition furthers the link between two places. A mask that will hold the gaze of a single person reminds us of the power of solitary experience. We have translated two masks into one: the inner form and fit of a Venetian mask, and the outer framing of a single broad slot that Australians will recognise as the

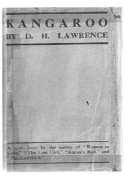

DH Lawrence, *Kangaroo*, London, Martin Secker, 1923.

hand wrought steel mask of our bushranger hero Ned Kelly. Many of the works within Sidney Nolan's Ned Kelly series illustrate the view of Australian landscape around and through the slot in Kelly's armoured mask. This is the point where those visiting the exhibition are invited to look within a vast cantilevering quilted timber portal, toward a cinematic representation of places within our buildings. These will merge, to suggest both specific and universal experiences of being within and passing through interior space.

At the time of writing, in February 2018, the construction of our exhibition *Somewhere Other* is nearing completion. It is to be disassembled and packed into a huge shipping container that will transport it to Venice. The same craftsmen who have fabricated and assembled it in Australia will meet it on arrival and reassemble it within the Arsenale. We hope that visitors to the Biennale will be drawn toward its various portals, to find themselves upside down and at the bottom of the world.

Jacaranda Industries
&
Tensys
&
Derek John

MAKING
SOMEWHERE
OTHER

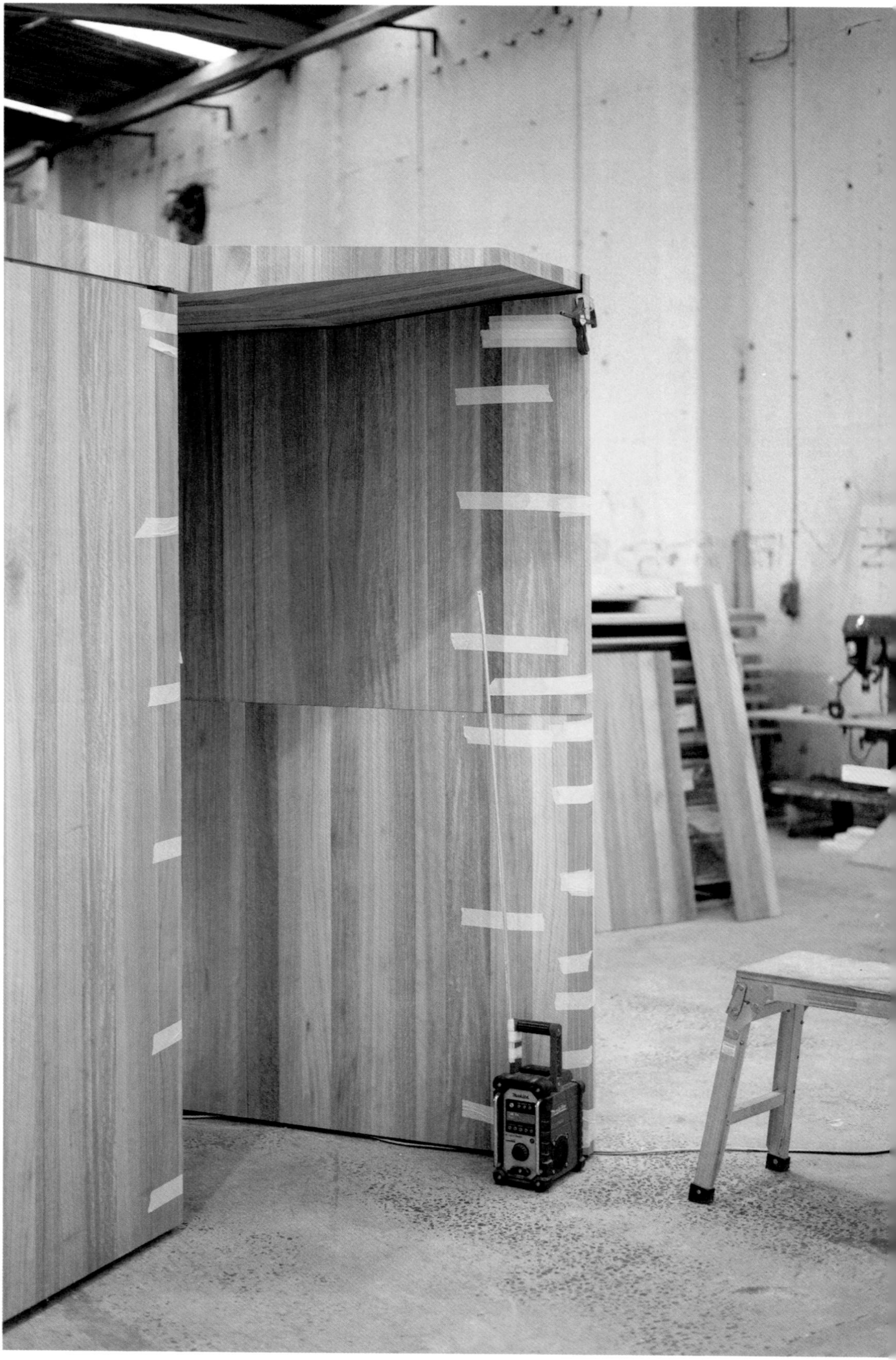

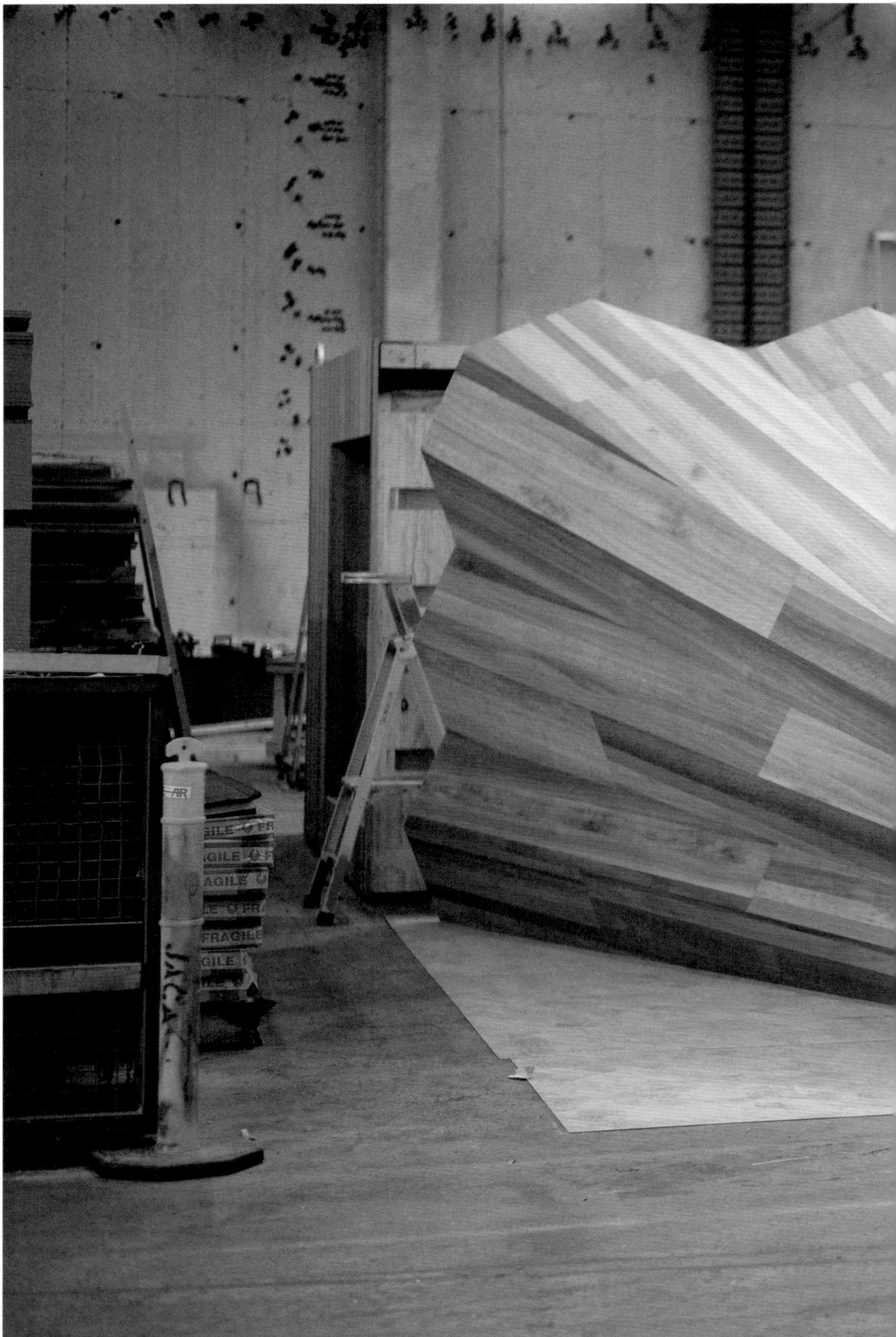
FRAGILE

Photographed
by
Trevor Mein

PICTURING SOMEWHERE OTHER

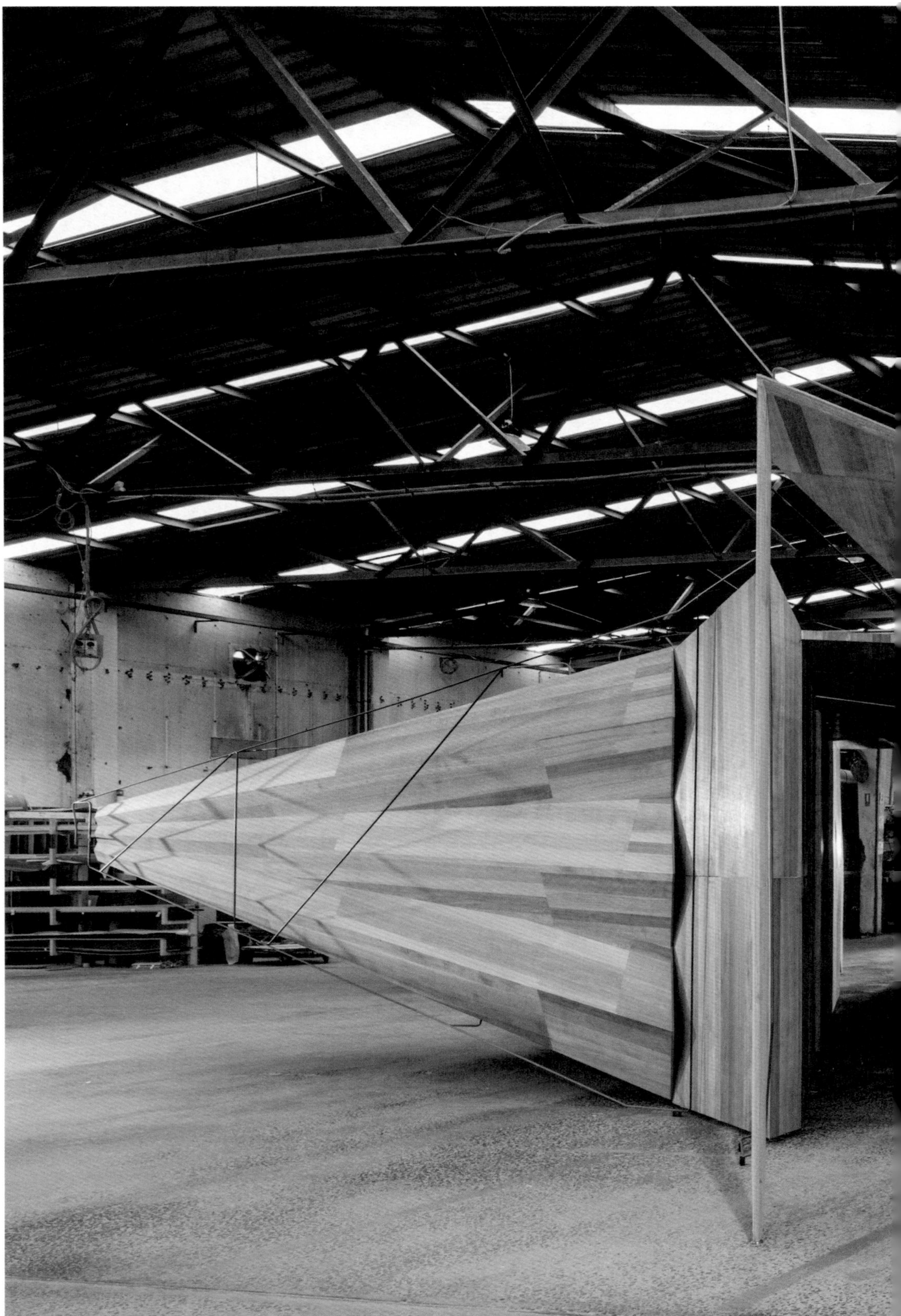

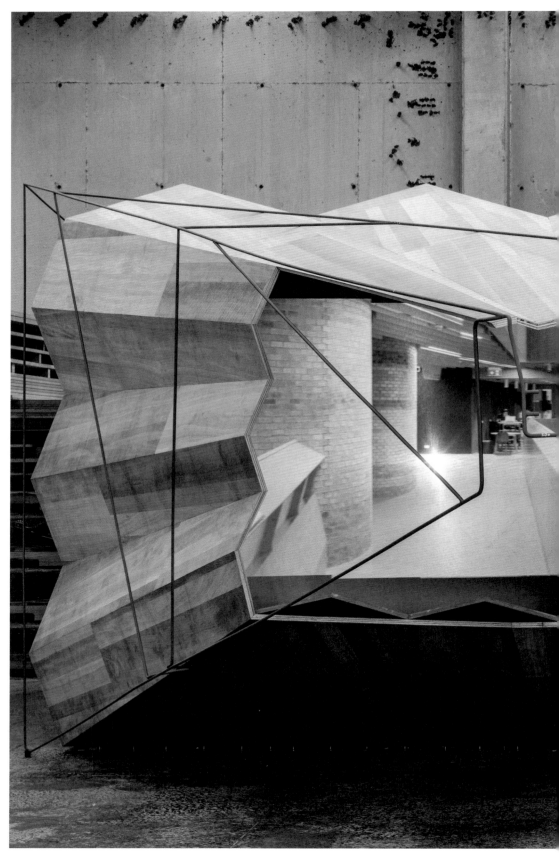

John Wardle
Architects
&
Friends

WORKS
MAKE
FRIENDS

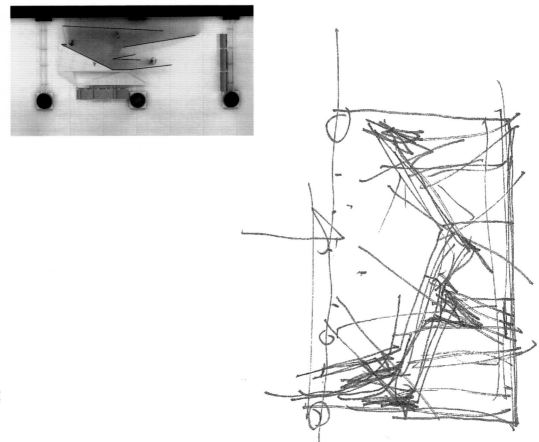

Our initial proposal was to construct the object that we created as a speculation for our tapestry, *Perspectives on a Flat Surface,* and erect it in the Arsenale. It refers to the extended perspectives of Palladio and Scamozzi's Teatro Olimpico and suggests long views to other places.

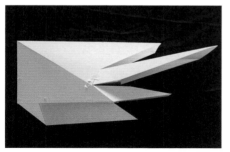

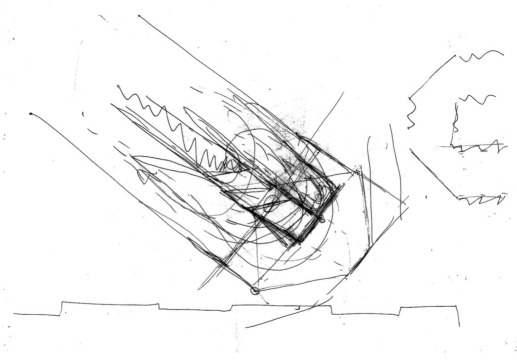

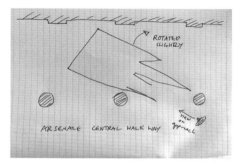

In discussion with Natasha Johns-Messenger over a series of workshops our scheme became more instrument-like, with portals that provide both apertures for engagement and surrounding armature for projected film.

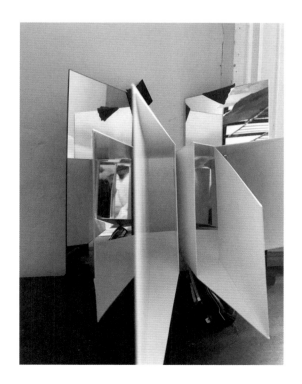

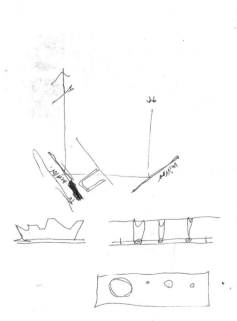

OBSERVER & PARTICIPANT

The film could follow many directions. Our work explores the nature of the portal, its relationship to the interior and the view, the space in-between, and the possibility of a thin cut or a thickened space of occupation. This may lead to revelation as a building's cross-section is made transparent or to intrigue when layering of a window protects it from the Antipodean sun. We consider what lies between the spectacle and the spectator, the difference between observer and participant. The portal freely offers the possibility of unexpected delight, a profound clarity of understanding, or an intimate adjacency.

This exploration of the portal is often intertwined with a consideration of landscape, and the viewer's relationship to it. We are often working within a landscape that has been constructed and altered over time. How does the viewer relate to this landscape through the device of the window?

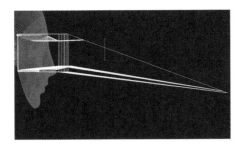

Different possibilities for the film:

SHEARERS QUARTERS – the portal as cinematic framing device of landscape (concealed frame, clipped view, hilly topography, thinly sliced).

CAPTAIN KELLY'S COTTAGE – the portal as a means to measure landscape (paned window frames, panelised view, beach cove, thickened with daybed).

LEARNING AND TEACHING BUILDING – the screened portal as memory of landscape (perforated screen, bark texture, radial scallops, layered to control light) and the brick tower window as a portal overlooking an interior constructed landscape of ravines and escarpments, the latest layer over the original indigenous landscape (bush, farming, campus, mat building).

NIGEL PECK CENTRE – portals as a giant ashlar pattern (foliage frit pattern, extruded steel portals extending toward view of the Domain and Botanic Gardens).

BONEO HOUSE – portals divine the view, the house is like a divining rod seeking the panorama (skewed and cranked in plan, splitting the view, detached and telescopic in the landscape).

FAIRHAVEN HOUSE – the portal as a release point (uncoiling the view, choreographed from vertical to horizontal, from below the tea tree to looking over it).

MELBOURNE CONSERVATORIUM OF MUSIC – the portal as a glimpse (a concentrated moment, circular, bell shaped, acoustically thickened, scaled to a person, scaled to a room, scaled to a street).

MELBOURNE SCHOOL OF DESIGN – the portal as history (neo-classical openings, perspectival interior desire lines, Teatro Olimpico, Palladio and Scamozzi, forced perspective, Joseph Reed's nose, inhabited façade).

KEW HOUSE – the portal as a surface (a cut end, glass suspended, reflective and transparent, private and public, a theatre of inhabitation).

LAKE WENDOUREE HOUSE – the portal as a figure (tracing the landscape, a built moment, inhabiting the in-between, a seam).

Or, more simply, the portals could be described as 'sliced', 'thickened', 'layered', 'unfolded', 'extruded', 'inhabited', 'figured' and 'branched'.

—Stefan Mee

64

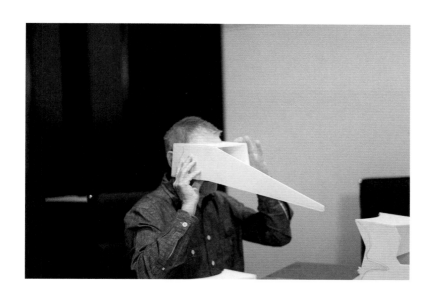

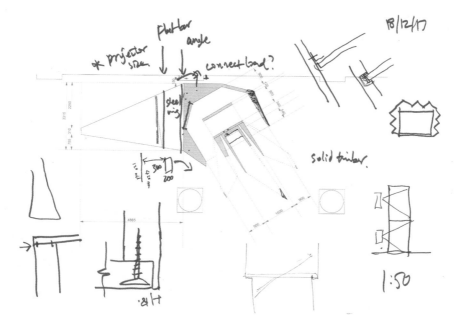

18/12/17

projector
side

flutter
angle

connect load?

steel
rig

solid timber

1:50

The viewing 'mask', for the perfect single-point perspective view into the long cantilevered chamber, combines the anthropomorphic fit of a Venetian mask and the broad aperture of the slot in Ned Kelly's bushranger's armour.

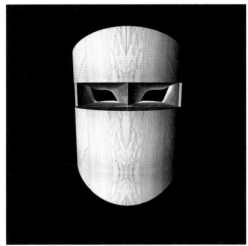

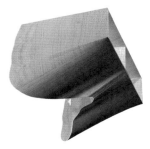

On 14 Feb 2018, at 3:02 am,
Francesca Giubilei

Dear John,

Here I am with more news about the glass object you asked to produce in Venice.

First of all I have to say that Muranese glass makers are not used to work on such big scale and the piece is not easy to realize.

In any case there are some considerations to do:
— we need to build a wooden mold to blown glass inside it and have a piece as much precise as possible, according with shape and size you gave us.
— the colour you selected "red" is a problematic one in glass, because it can change a lot during the cooking. So we don't have any certainty about the final result, it could be good but could be also very dark or not uniform. For this reason the glass maker suggested to use an amber colour, which is between orange-yellow and light brown. A very beautiful colour I have to say!
— finally a very important question for you: are the dimensions of the piece you gave us very strict? To blow a piece of 1m with a diameter of 43cm is very risky and difficult. The glass master told me that he will be able to blow 90cm long and 35cm of diameter for sure.

What do you think about this option?

Looking forward to hearing from you, so that we can go ahead with the process and send you a final estimate according with your decision.

Francesca

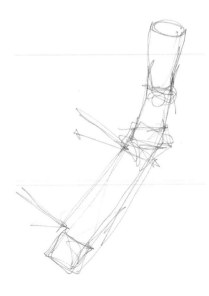

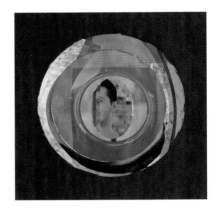

From: John Wardle
Date: 14 February 2018 at 8:29:49am
To: Francesca Giubilei
Cc: Alan Ting, James Loder
Subject: Re: GLASS PIECE PRODUCTION FOR VENICE BIENNALE

Dear Francesca,

I'm pleased to hear from you. Firstly I'm very happy to work with you and the glass master to better appreciate the parameters of the process that he will employ to make this.

The colour sounds fine, in fact it is meant to be orange not red so this outcome will be perfect. The intention was to match the colour of a tapestry that we have designed that is many shades of orange. I will send you an image of it. Please don't worry if the colour is uneven as I can imagine it to be beautiful if the colour and translucency vary along its length.

Your dimensions are fine and can vary again during production if this takes the pressure off you both. I would like however the wider end to be as large as he can form it. Much less than 35cm would be a pity as I'd like its conical profile to be emphasised. I will send you the original sketch I did for this which may assist with shaping the mould.

We will match the form achieved with our steelwork.

This is very exciting. I greatly look forward to hearing back from you and in May visiting you and the glass master's workshop.

My best wishes
John

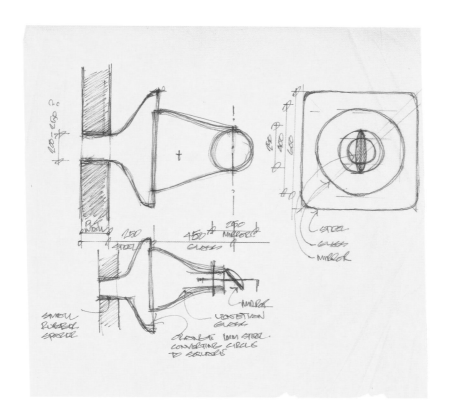

The 'Venetian Portal' that accepts the view out from within the chamber has been fabricated by Glass Master Leonardo Cimolin in Murano.

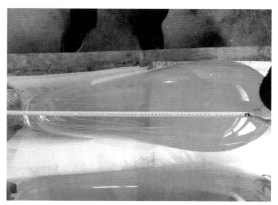

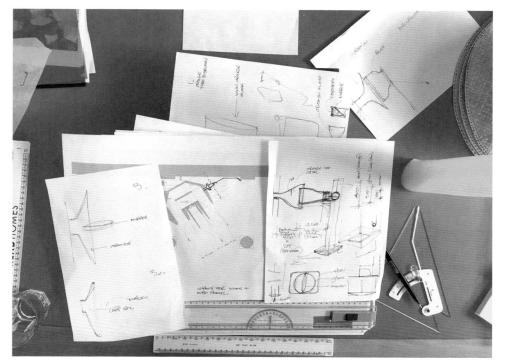

The inserted conical opening in the chamber wall refers to our series of windows set into massive precast concrete panels that will provide views from the street frontage into the Music Studio of our Conservatorium of Music currently under construction in Melbourne.

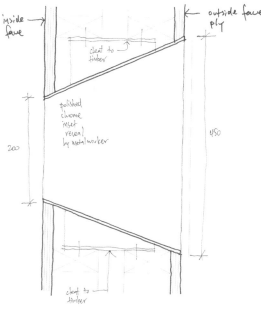

CHROME INSERT
1:2 @A3
JWA VENICE

5.2.2018

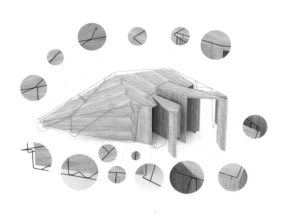

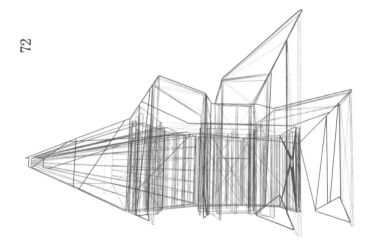

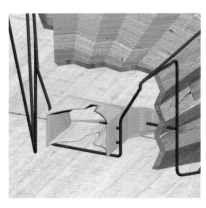

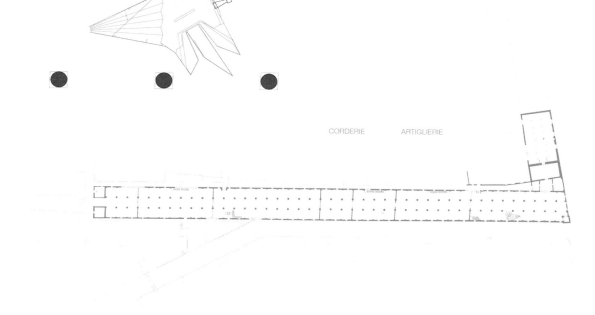

CORDERIE   ARTIGLIERIE

The structure has been dismantled and packed into sixteen boxes that fit into two shipping containers bound for Venice.

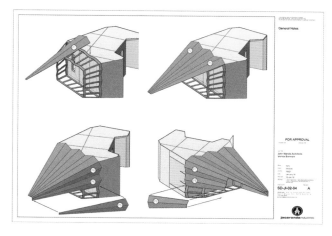

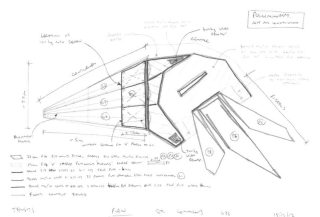

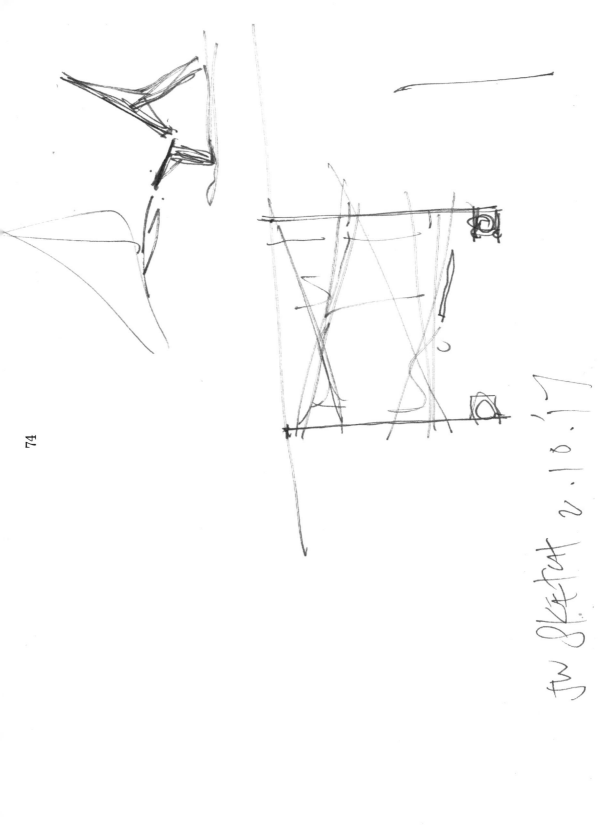

74

JW Sketch 2.16.17

Natasha
        Johns-
Messenger

ILLUSIONS
& ALLUSIONS

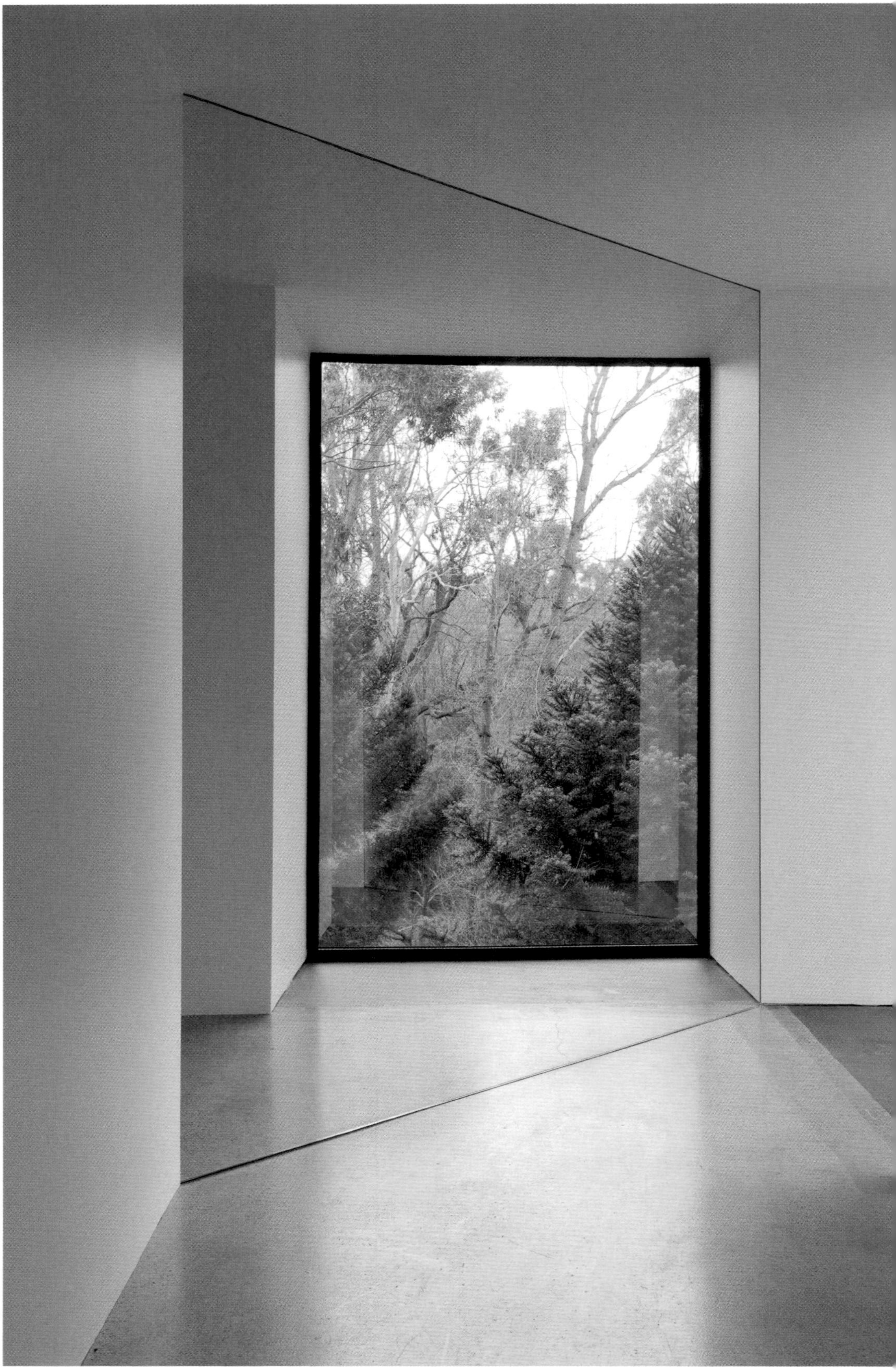

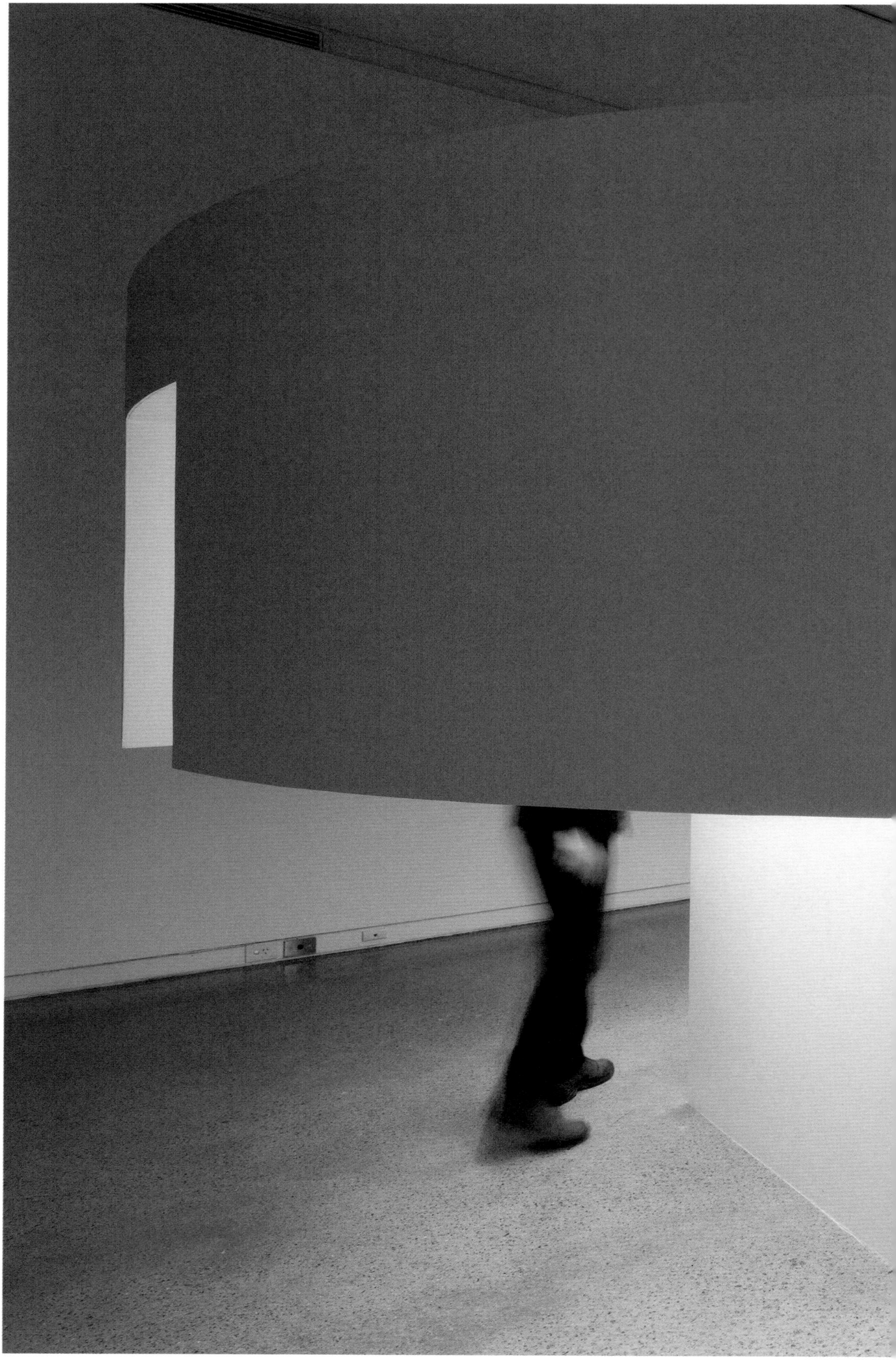

Coco
&
Maximilian

A FRACTURED
IMAGE

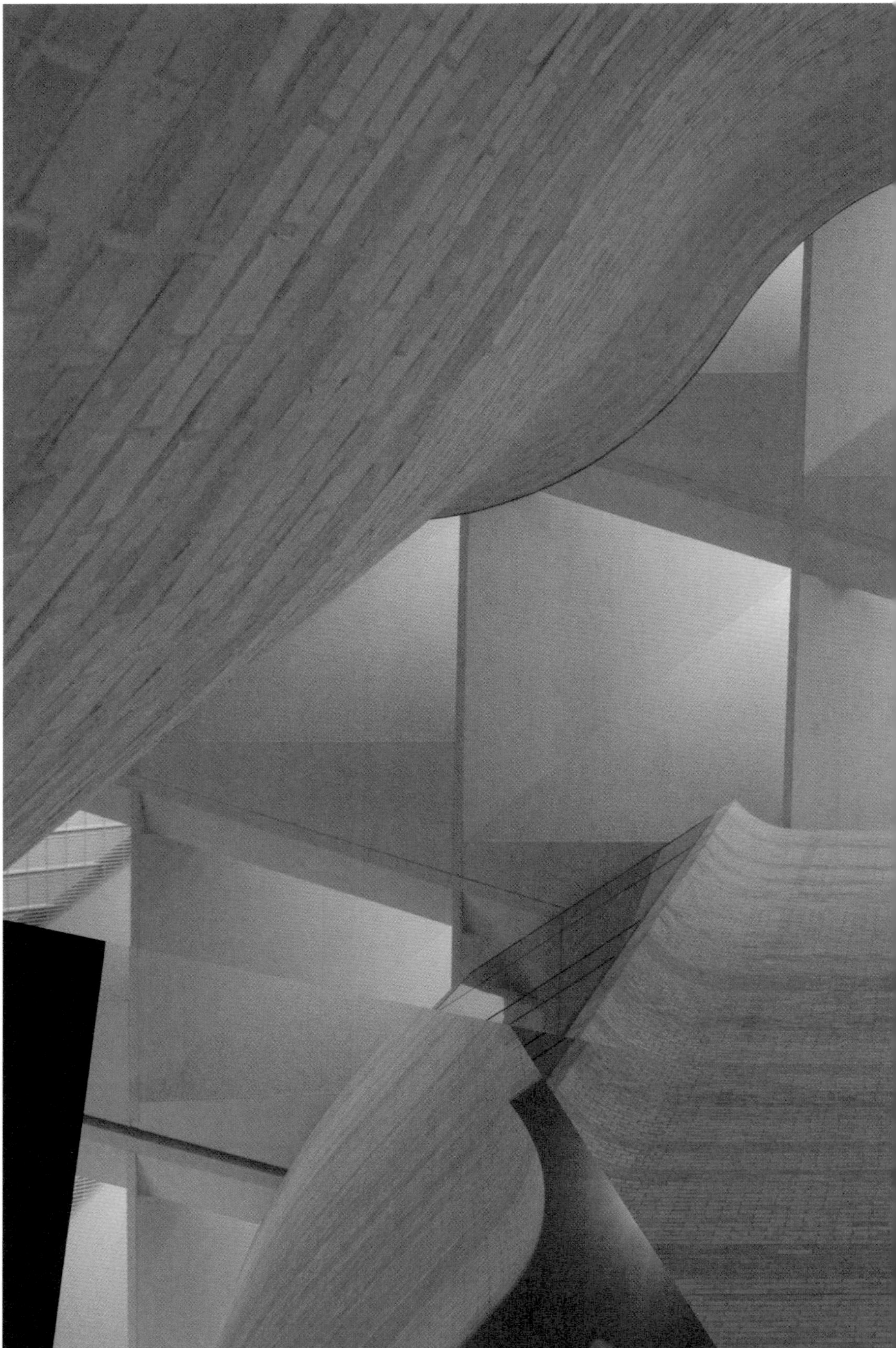

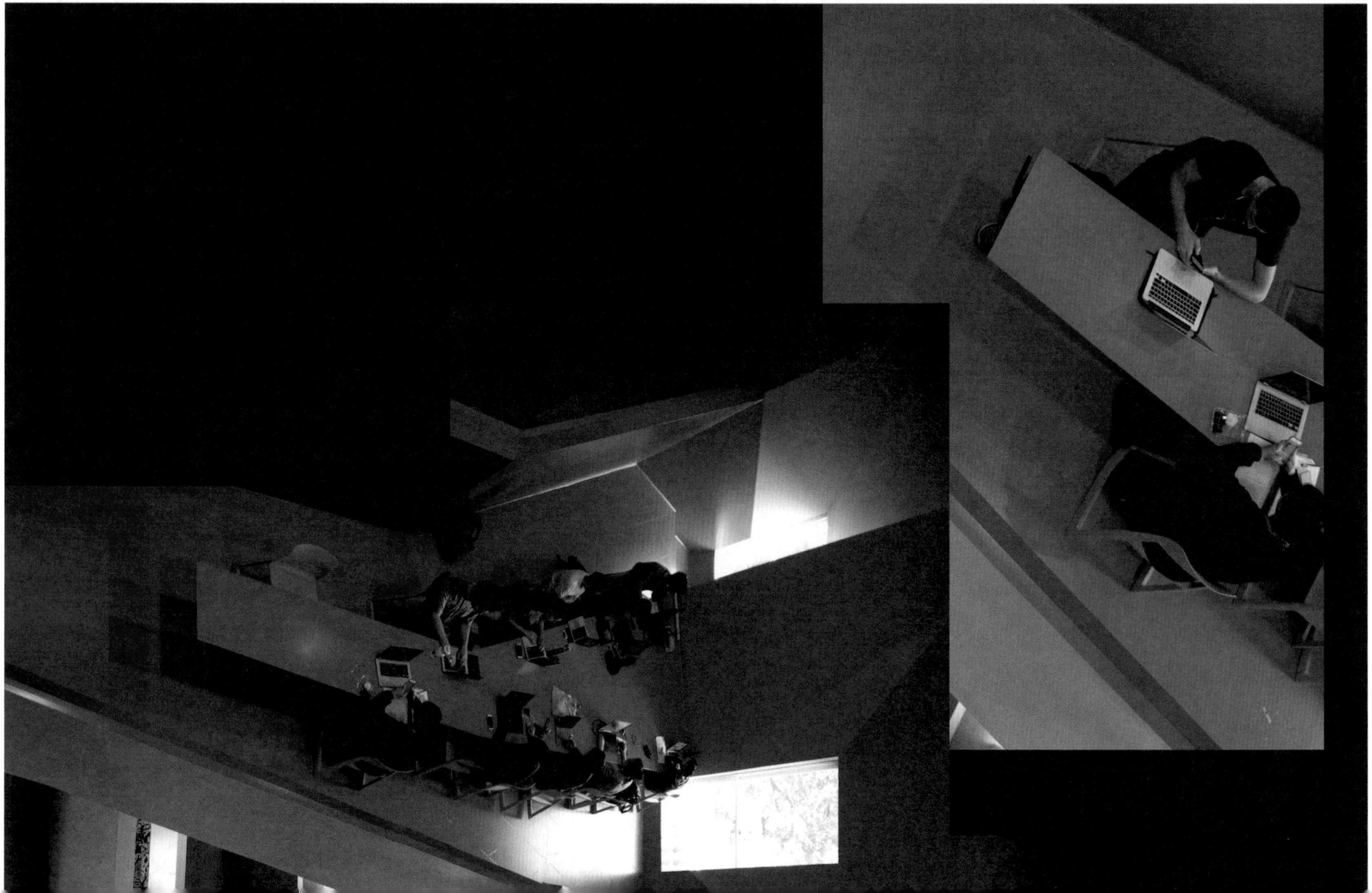

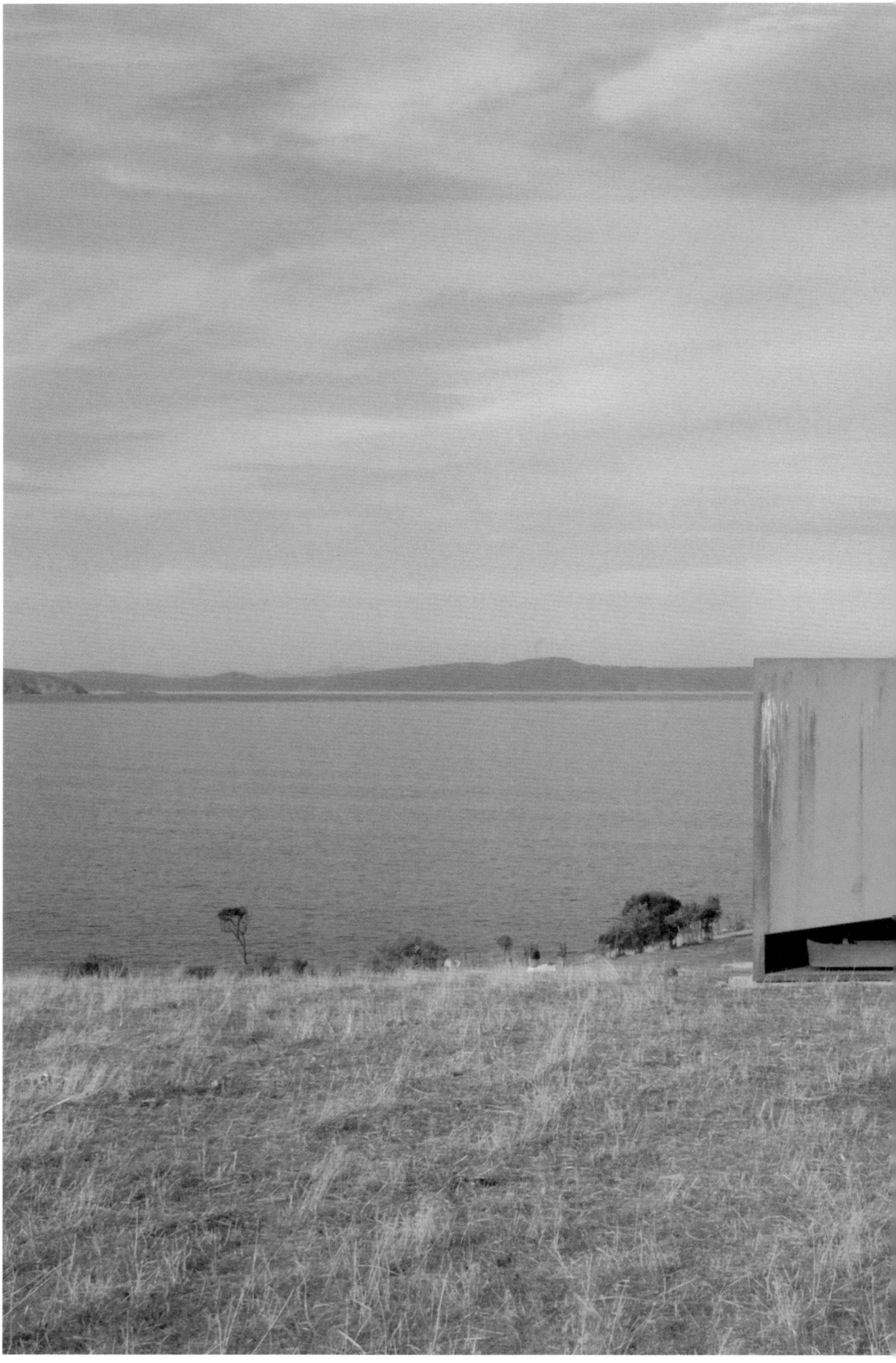

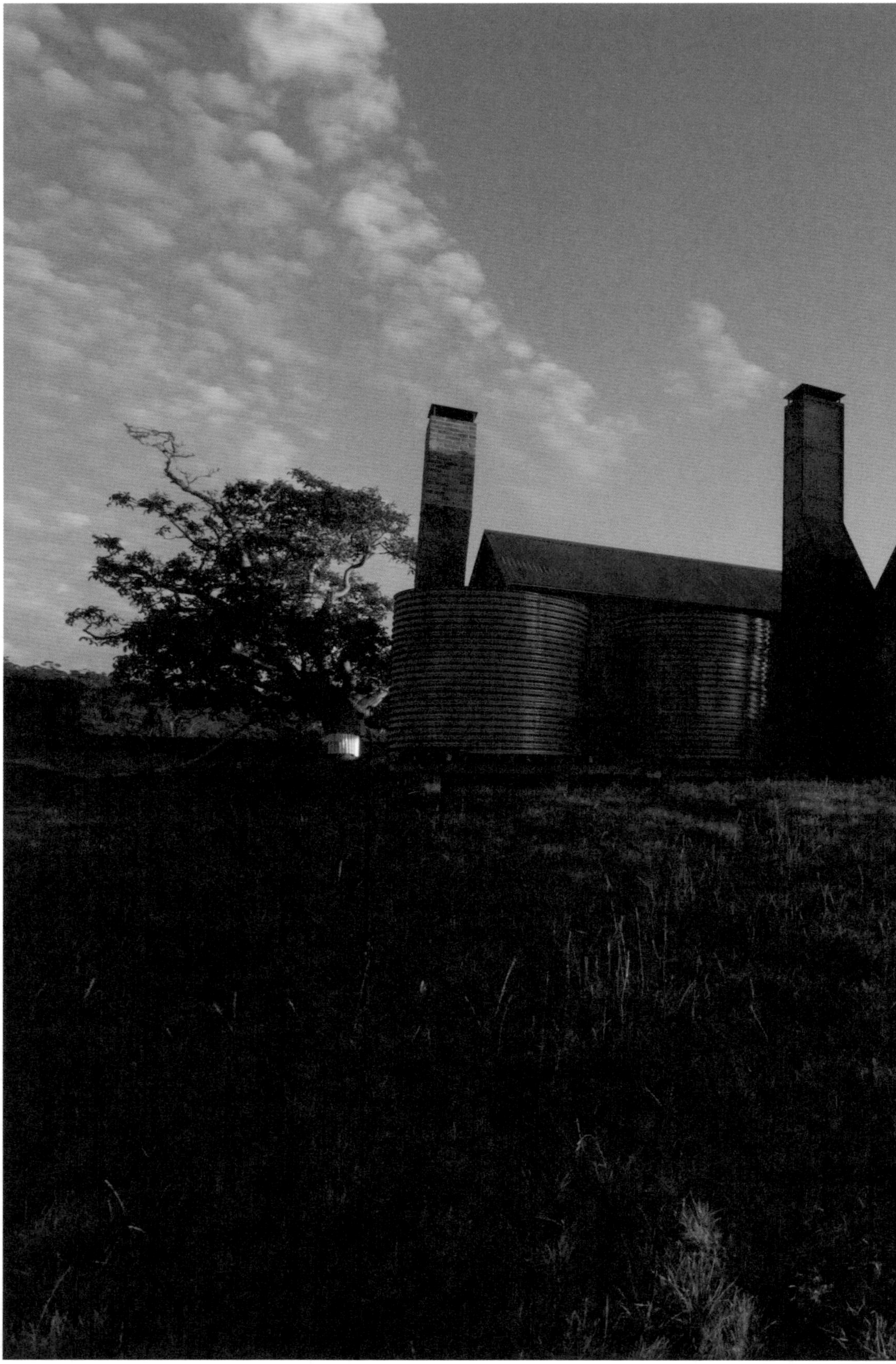

Australian Tapestry Workshop
&
Leonardo Cimolin

ON MAKING
OBJECTS

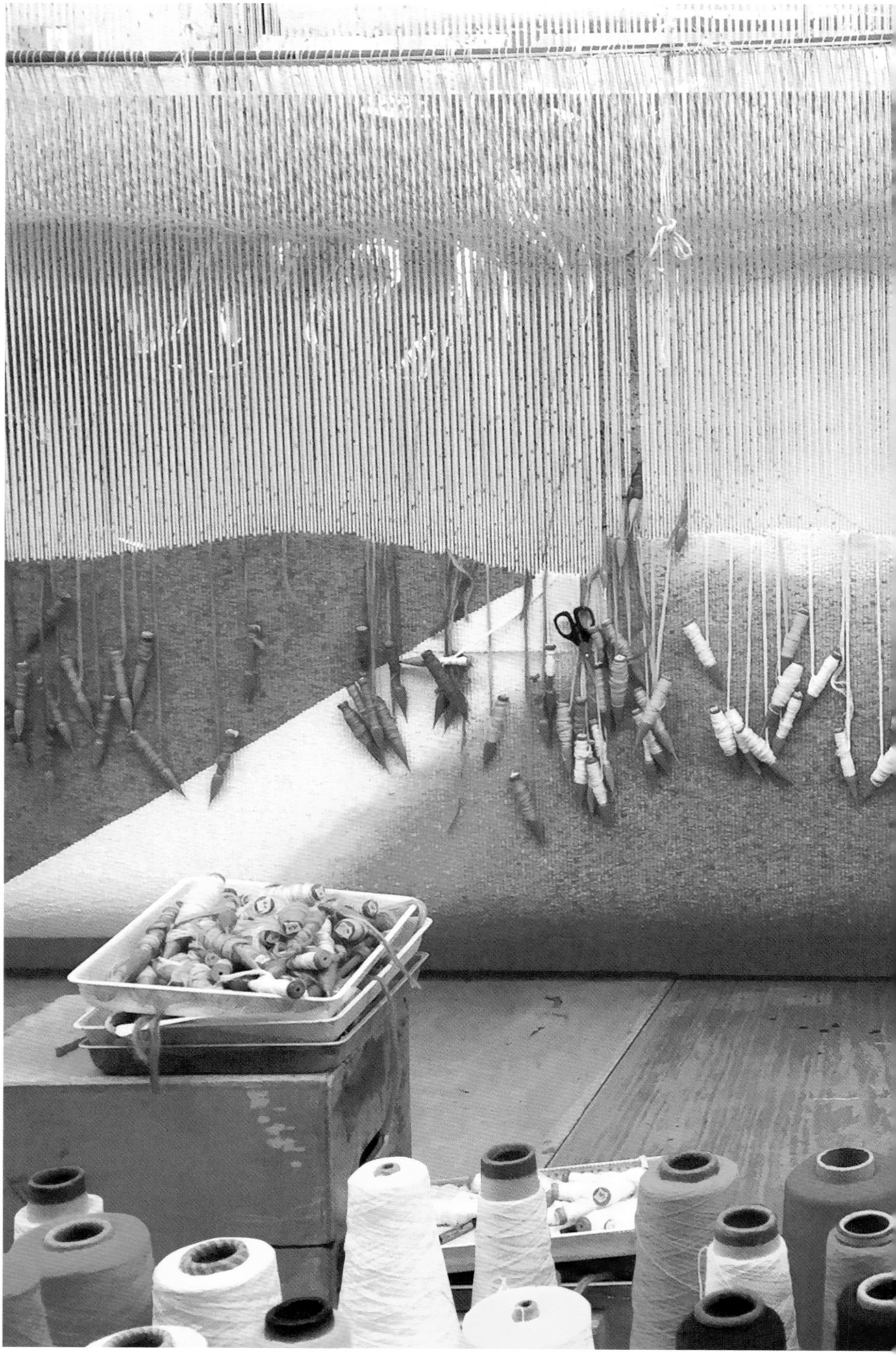

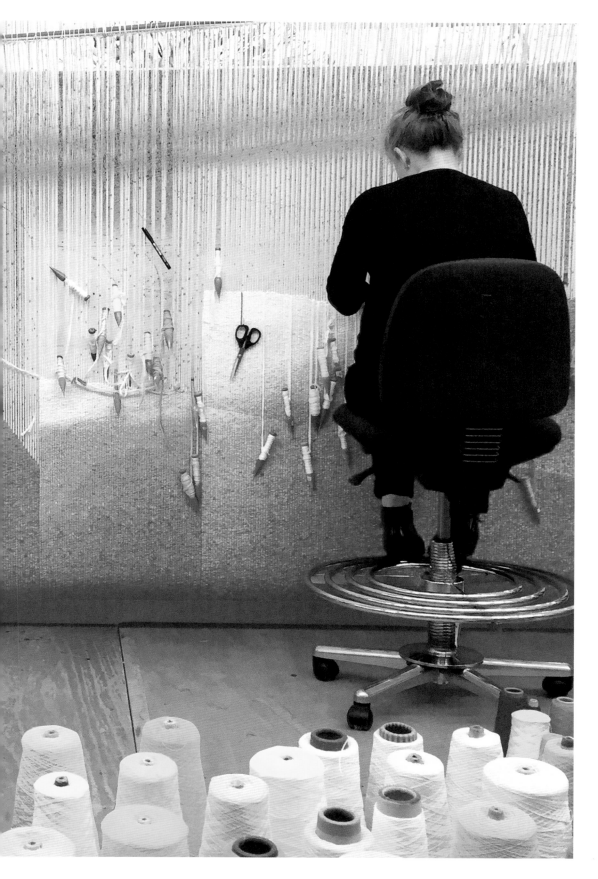

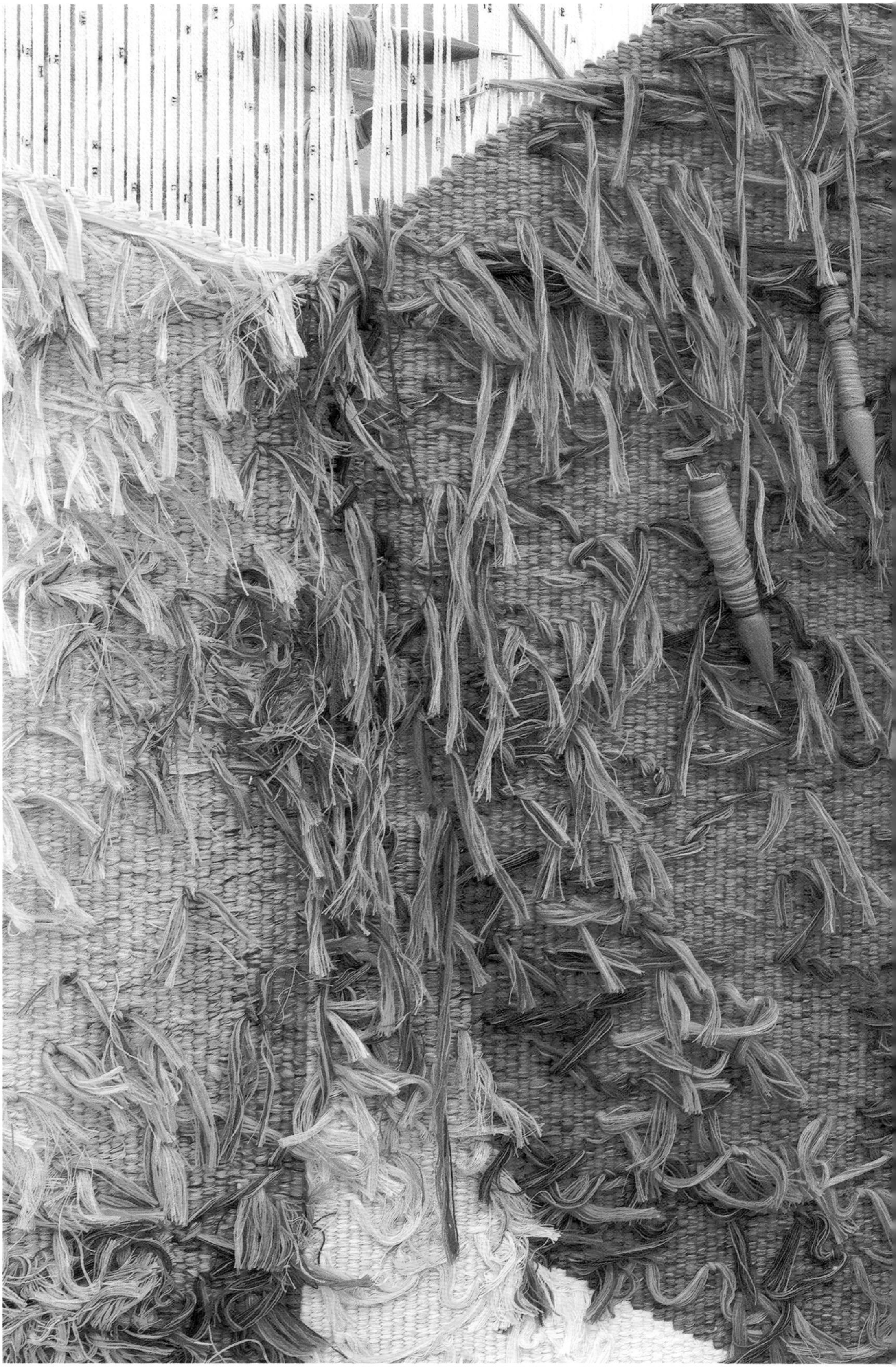

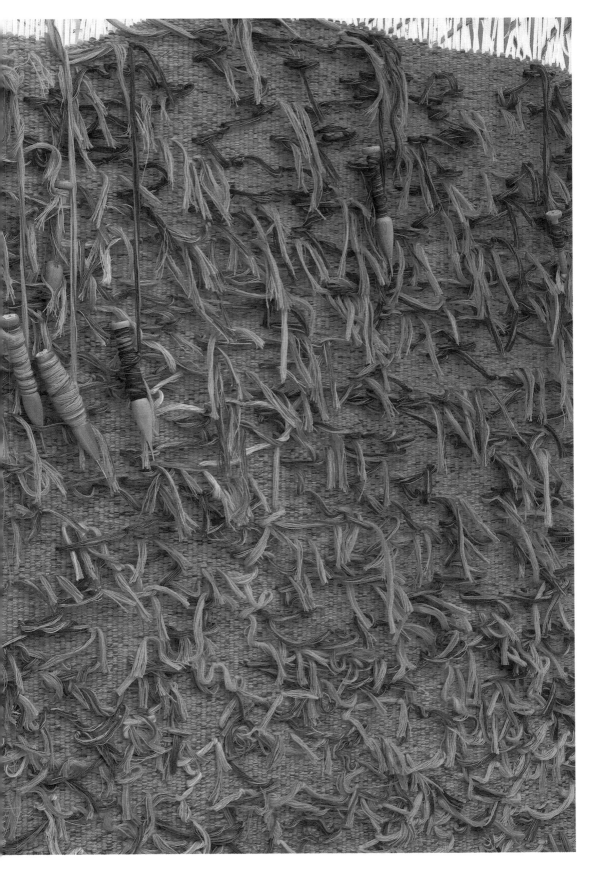

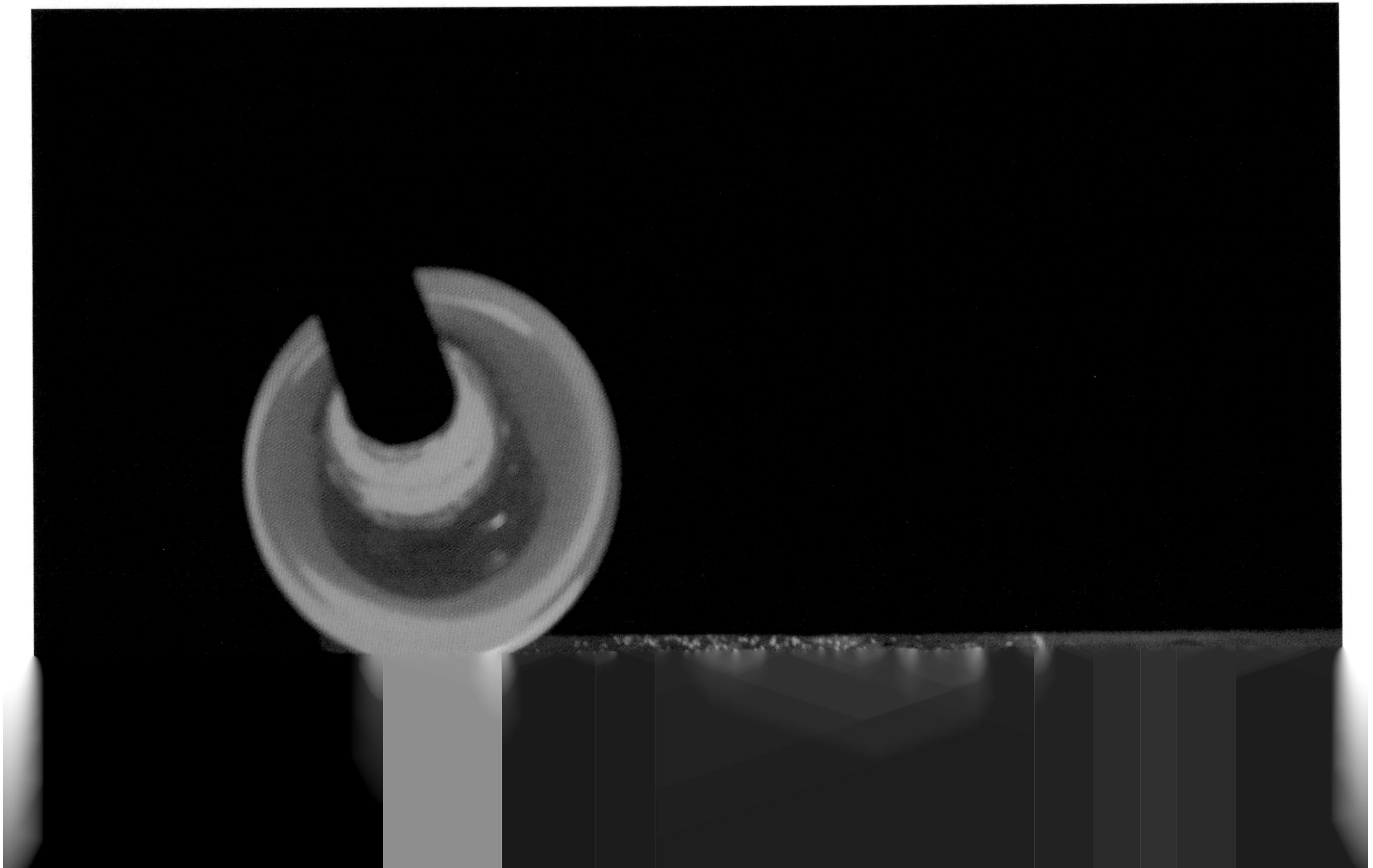

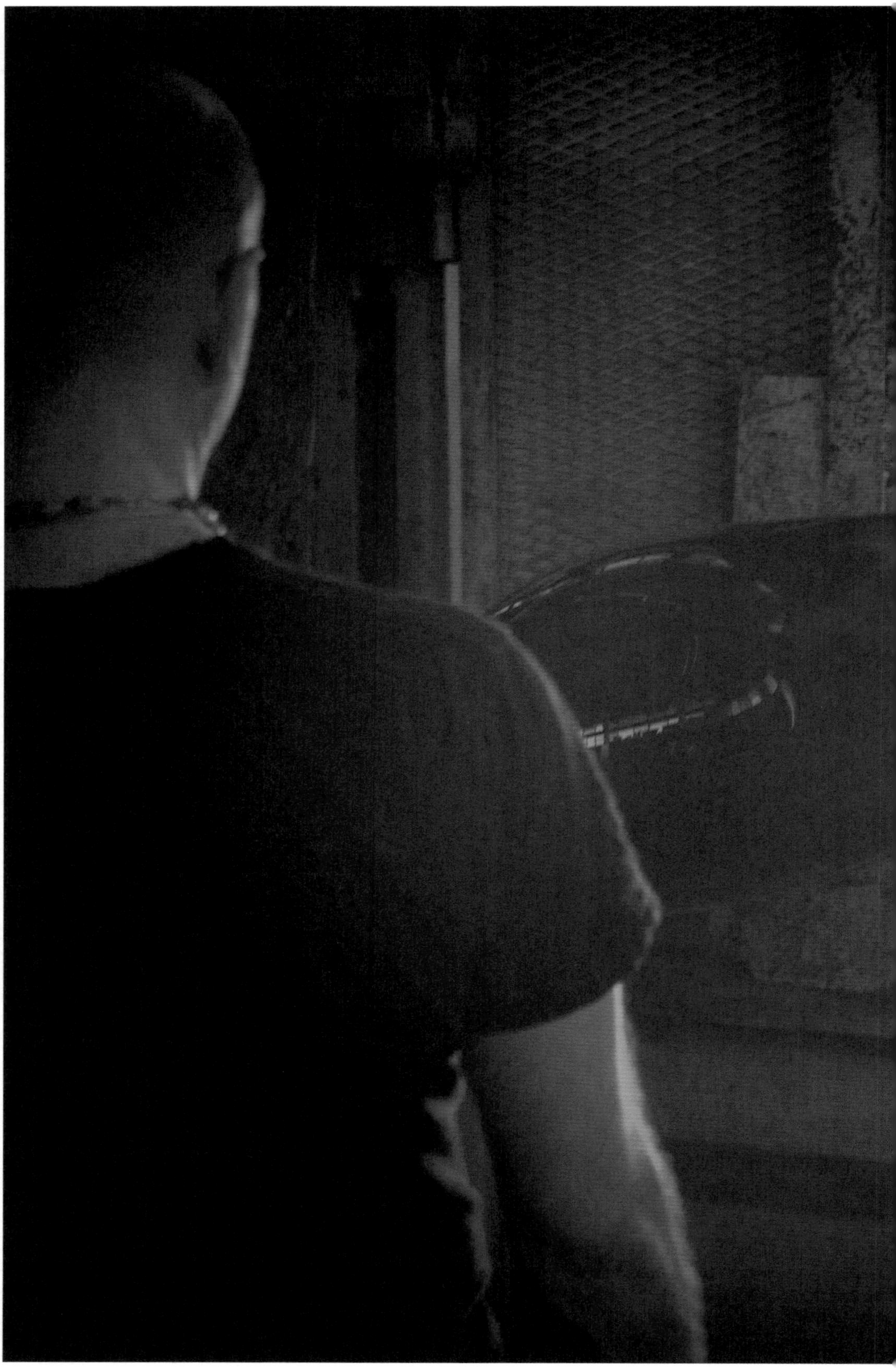

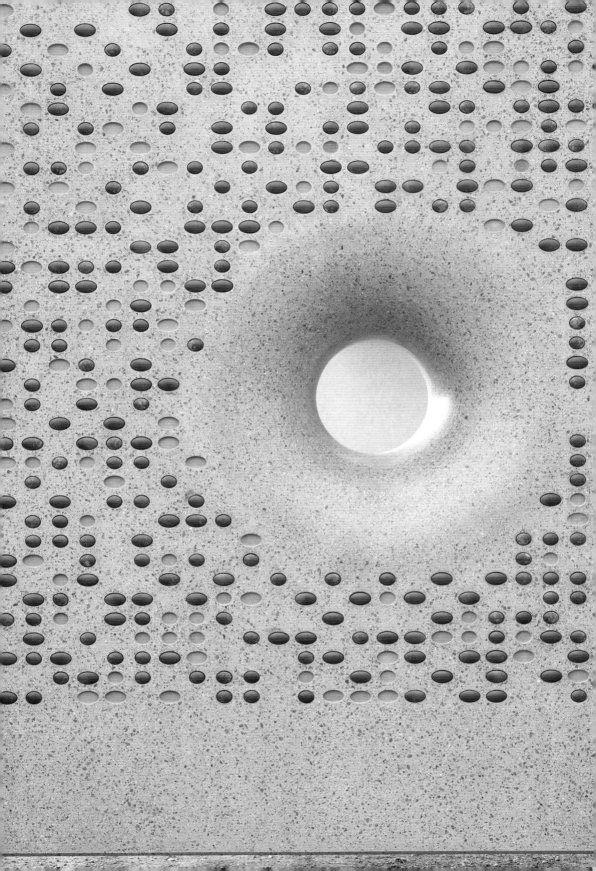

Rory
Hyde

OTHER
PORTALS

I am speaking to John Wardle through a portal. A thread of glass fibre, draped underneath the ocean, connects my study in London to his in Melbourne. Like a window pane that has been liquefied and stretched to form an expanded threshold. We are speaking on Skype, a piece of commercial software that conceals the magnitude of this activity. I am drinking coffee, he is drinking wine, while our conversation is conveyed at close to the speed of light between our computers on opposite sides of the Earth. A banal miracle of the 21st century.

 We are talking about portals. In particular, John Wardle Architects' proposal for the 16th International Architecture Exhibition of the Venice Biennale, which establishes a portal between Venice and Australia. It is a paradoxical thing, part telescope, and part gateway, simultaneously reaching upward, while being pulled out into a long cantilevered tube. Constructed in timber, and framed by steel, it bears both the marks of handicraft, and the geometry of the digital. Stretched, as if by perspective, it is simultaneously large and small, heavy and light, neither building nor furniture, model or artwork, but something *other*.

 Titled 'Somewhere Other', being 'other' is central to the work. This slippery phrase defines what it is not, or rather, *where* it is not.

Made in the regional city of Geelong, it has been disassembled and packed into shipping containers, and re-assembled in Venice. From its place in the Arsenale, amid the dim light, humid heat, red-brick walls and circular columns, a portal is opened up with its origins in Australia. Films recording moments with various JWA projects are framed by the structure, embedded within it, extending the view through and beyond to another continent. "Upside-down at the bottom of the world", as DH Lawrence described Australia in 1922, a description which Wardle cites as a starting point. And yet this is another phrase that defines what is not, rather than what is. So what is this work Wardle has created?

"It is an instrument", he tells me. "An instrument of extending space." This word - foreign to architecture - conjures up both the scientific and the musical. A thing carefully calibrated to serve a specific purpose, even if that purpose may be to entertain, or to create an experience. This is something that could be said of much of JWA's work, dancing between the calculated and the whimsical, the pragmatic and the enjoyable. *Somewhere Other* is a kind of synthesis of these tendencies in earlier projects, distilled to an essence.

The materiality speaks to the firm's fascination with joinery. The bits where the body rubs up against the building, and architecture

Cabinetry at Lake Wendouree Residence.

Architecture becoming furniture at Captain Kelly's Cottage.

becomes furniture. When visiting a JWA building, it can often feel as though the cabinets were conceived on day one, as if that's really all they wanted to do. Here, timber has been teased into pleats and frames, arches and masks, in gestures that continually ask more of the material, and more of the makers. "We are a firm of architects who inhabit factories", says Wardle, to emphasise the breaking down of the assumed boundaries – of class, of taste – between the designer and the fabricator. "You don't have to get to know these people", he says, "but we do". The joiners, Jacaranda Industries, are behind JWA's most expressive moments, such as the suspended timber room in the atrium of the Melbourne School of Design building at the University of Melbourne. Their dedication to this project is such that a small team will be flown out to Venice to oversee installation.

But most of all *Somewhere Other* speaks to the firm's fascination with framing of views and of landscape. The projects are instruments of looking, of alignments with features or moments. This is most evident in JWA's houses, in particular one of Wardle's own houses on Bruny Island in Tasmania, the Shearers Quarters. Wardle describes how this house was sited and how the plan evolved as a process of investigation and 'orchestration' - another musical term. An inlet, a woolshed, a

Prototype models for the Shearers Quarters.

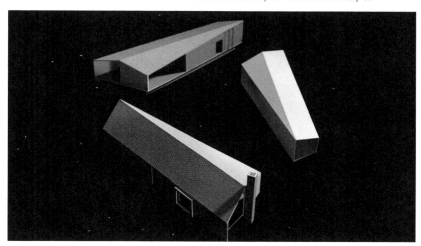

peak, a field, all become origins of vectors which drive the plan. Threads which are pulled from the distance into the domestic, setting up relationships between inside and out. "We shrink-wrap the view", says Wardle, "we compartmentalised it, not so you say 'gee whiz', but to disrupt it and reveal it cinematically". The windows – the portals – become the central tools of this orchestration: projecting, revealing, aligning with these vectors beyond.

This function of the Shearer's Quarters as an instrument of looking is conveyed most succinctly by Trevor Mein's iconic photographs, where the eye is drawn past the house to rest on the landscape. We are not really looking at the building at all, but at the link it establishes with what's outside it. It's worth stating that this is not normally how we consider architecture. We are conditioned to look at the thing itself, not past it or through it. But in a way that is the

generosity of JWA's work, it invites you not (just) to revere the object, but to be connected to a context, and the narratives it contains.

And yet, unlike the rolling hills and sparkling seas of Tasmania's Bruny Island, the Arsenale is a paradoxical site for such a portal. It is a space defined by its interiority, relentless in its length, with little connection to the world beyond. Wandering through the Biennale exhibits, it's easy to forget where you are, only to step out into the blinding light of the lagoon, blinking. Again, Wardle revels in this contradiction. The constraints of the site are used to amplify the illusion of the portal. In collaboration with the artist Natasha Johns-Messenger, Coco & Maximilian's films within the structure are framed in a single-point perspective, creating a sight-line that extends beyond the walls of the Arsenale. This trick breaks through the wall, without knocking out a single brick, emphasising the sense of reaching beyond its footprint, and back to its origin in Australia.

In this sense *Something Other* seems to point beyond itself. It seems to say, "yes, look at this thing sitting here, look at its shape and how it is made. But more importantly, look through it and past it, and look at where it's come from". And surely that's the purpose of the Venice Biennale, to offer up these instruments of connection in an

Left: a view from the Shearers Quarters.

Rory Hyde is a designer, curator and writer based in London. His work is focused on new forms of design practice, and redefining the role of the designer today. He is Curator of Contemporary Architecture and Urbanism at the Victoria and Albert Museum, Adjunct Senior Research Fellow at the University of Melbourne, and Design Advocate for the Mayor of London.

attempt to tie the disparate threads together, in order that we may learn from one another, and push the discipline forward.

As our Skype conversation winds up, and we say our goodbyes, a sound from outside jumps down the line. It's the unmistakable gravelly whistle of a wattlebird, a sound ignored by Wardle, but which lands straight on my heart. I'm knocked off balance, struck by homesickness, and all the indescribable emotions that a single bird call can dredge up. I can feel the portal sucking me in, calling me home, reminding me of all the pieces I've left behind, the pieces of me that are somewhere other.

Max
Delany

APERTURES, PORTALS & THE FRAMING OF SOMEWHERE OTHER

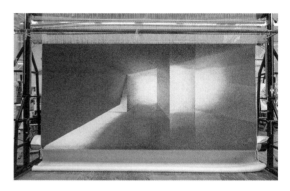

John Wardle
Architects' tapestry
*Perspectives on a
Flat Surface.*

The generosity of spirit, the offering of spatial gifts, and the resourceful deployment of light, space, air and gravity that Yvonne Farrell and Shelley McNamara emphasise at the outset of their Freespace manifesto might have been written with John Wardle Architects (JWA) in mind – the Australian architectural practice known for its material craft, social engagement, lightness of touch and spatio-temporal playfulness.
        JWA's *Somewhere Other*, developed at the invitation of Farrell and McNamara, is an architectural installation designed in collaboration with an artist, film-makers, artisans and engineers. The installation is extrapolated from and presented in dialogue with a previous work by the studio in 2016, mural-scale tapestry *Perspectives on a Flat Surface*. Both works are propositions of architecture in the sense that their physical structures are secondary to the ideas and experiences they present. Indeed, *Somewhere Other* is described as more akin to an 'instrument' than 'architecture' by the architect. Its status as architectural proposition or sketch is first elaborated as a steel frame drawing in space, underscoring the conceptual or schematic nature of the project. The instrument itself is constructed with an internal timber frame clad in spotted gum, an Australian native hardwood, which was dispatched from Melbourne to the ship-building headquarters of the Veneto.

Inserted into the structure are a series of screen-like mirrors and films – by artist Natasha Johns-Messenger and film-makers Coco and Maximilian respectively – and an optical device. Each element emphasises the subjective, illusory nature of architectural experience and the choreography of bodies in space. In this complex tripartite structure, JWA stages the drama and contest of the material, spatial and social dimensions that lie at the heart of its practice.

As a series of lenses or apertures onto architecture and the world, *Somewhere Other* is constructivist in form. The piece is a sequence of rushing, turning and returning perspectives, which reflect the athleticism of JWA's architectural practice. John Wardle's theory of 'crush and release', which underscores his studio's working methodology[1], might just as aptly describe this work. As a quasi-pavilion exploded in plan, *Somewhere Other* is characterised by an elasticity of form and dimension, dynamically contracting and expanding from intimate to public scale. This shift in small to large spaces serves to emphasise the relationship of the individual to the civic community – a compression and expansion which metaphorically extends from Australia to Europe, and from solitary perception in the present to the collective experience of public space and history.

1.
John Wardle, 'Leading from the Middle', in John Wardle Architects, *This Building Likes Me*, Thames and Hudson, Port Melbourne, 2016, p.34.

2.
Natasha Johns-Messenger's mirrored intervention achieves the appearance of a long shaft of light that recalls the long corridor that dissects the ground floor plan of JWA's Queenscliff House (2005-2010).

Johns-Messenger is one of a number of artists with whom JWA has repeatedly collaborated with on past architectural projects. Well-known for her use of light, gravity, site and space to create illusory, perplexing architectural installations, Johns-Messenger has again been enlisted to shape and confound our experience of architecture. Her very simple introduction of two mirrors angled at the junctions of a U-shaped passageway acts as a powerful device to redefine the space – as if puncturing a hole through the architectural form and opening up the object to alternative spatial understandings.[2]

Upon entering the installation through a portal, we traverse an apparently long, narrow passage, which appears to extend deep into space and back out into the world. As we continue along this shaft-like threshold we encounter the mirror, only to be confronted by our own image, which we meet suddenly, and by surprise, in the reflective surface. Like the architectural cuts of Gordon Matta-Clark, which open up architecture to unexpected consequences and conditions, and the video feedback loops and real time image capture of Dan Graham's early two-way video and mirror installations, architecture and sculpture are opened to unexpected encounters. The collaboration of Johns-Messenger and JWA finds the intangible qualities of surprise and wonder associated with illusory modes of spatial perception and confusion, where simple axial configurations become labyrinthine, confounding, twisting and warping of space and place. This heightened perceptual experience induces an increased level of awareness in the beholder, a phenomenology which accords with the bodily, haptic and psychological experience of dwelling and inhabitation. Johns-Messenger's architectural cuttings, simulations and interruptions-in-space have been described by Melissa Bianca Amore as "optical prisms or spatial apertures ... that frame perception and the site as two inter-twining modalities."[3] As viewers we are witness to perception in action, in process. Our relationship to architecture, site and that which lies beyond is experienced consciously.

Another of the site's optical devices is a polished chrome cone embedded within a wall, which extends beyond the architecture through a funnel-shaped form blown from Venetian glass. The play between interior and exterior space is again elaborated, this time with reference to the figure of a mask, recalling two specific cultural reference points. One is Antipodean: the armoured steel mask of the bushranger Ned Kelly, as represented by the mid-twentieth-century modernist paintings of Sidney Nolan; and the other is the Venetian

3.
See Melissa Bianca Amore, 'The Mind as Architecture', in Linda Michael (ed.), *Sitelines: Natasha Johns-Messenger*, Heide Museum of Modern Art, Bulleen, 2017, p.18.

Left: Natasha Johns-Messenger's mirrors (left and right passage), with one of Coco and Maximilian's films (centre).

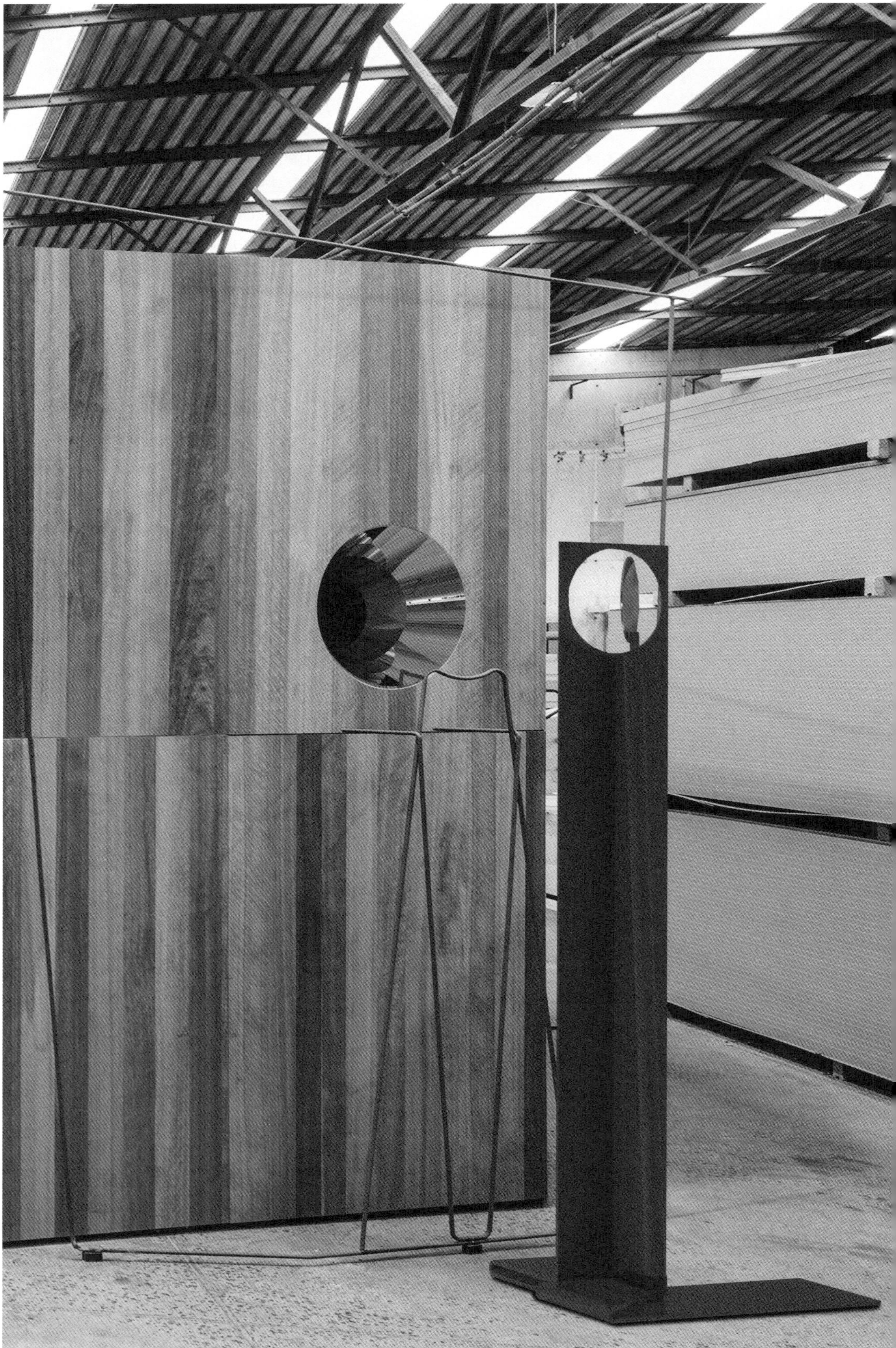

mask with its carnivalesque traditions and reference to modes of exhibition(ism). Nolan's paintings of Kelly and his geometric mask are now canonical examples of the ways in which European modernist abstraction was mapped onto the pictorial space of the Australian landscape. This uneasy confrontation underscores how the view of the colonial settler is disconnected from the landscape, how the imperial gaze is mediated by a form of European abstraction, and at odds with Indigenous perspectives which demonstrate an interconnectedness to landscape and Country. This sense of the portal or oculus is a recurrent motif in JWA's work. The portal serves to mediate between architecture, landscape and dwelling, while also referring to the lens of inherited cultural layers and persistent filtering of time and memory.

Another portal into the practice of JWA is apparent in the maze-like filmic journey of Coco and Maximilian. Presented across two screens – one portrait and one landscape – the films represent JWA's existing architecture in ways that are partial, emotional and experiential rather than documentative. Drawing on the way that film editing and photomontage work to encourage emotional as much as intellectual engagement, the film-makers capture the haptic experience of dwelling and habitation and the fugitive nature of

Left: the chrome cone in the side of the instrument, waiting for its Venetian glass.

Max Delany is Artistic Director and Chief Executive Officer of the Australian Centre for Contemporary Art, Melbourne, and adjunct Associate Professor, Curatorial Practice, in the Faculty of Art, Design and Architecture, Monash University.

memory. Their collaboration with JWA finds delight in the active life of architecture, recalling the Freespace manifesto. The choreography of the quotidian is celebrated in the pleasure of glimpses, feelings, sensations, materials and memories.

If the mirrored architectural slices of John Wardle Architects and Natasha Johns-Messenger concern our perception of the architectural pavilion space and Venetian Arsenale exhibition site, Coco and Maximilian's films return us back to the local and specifically Australian context of JWA's architecture. These are the dynamics that are elaborated in *Somewhere Other*: the relations between interior and exterior, between now and then, between the citizen and the body politic, the individual and the crowd, and between Australia, Europe and the world beyond.

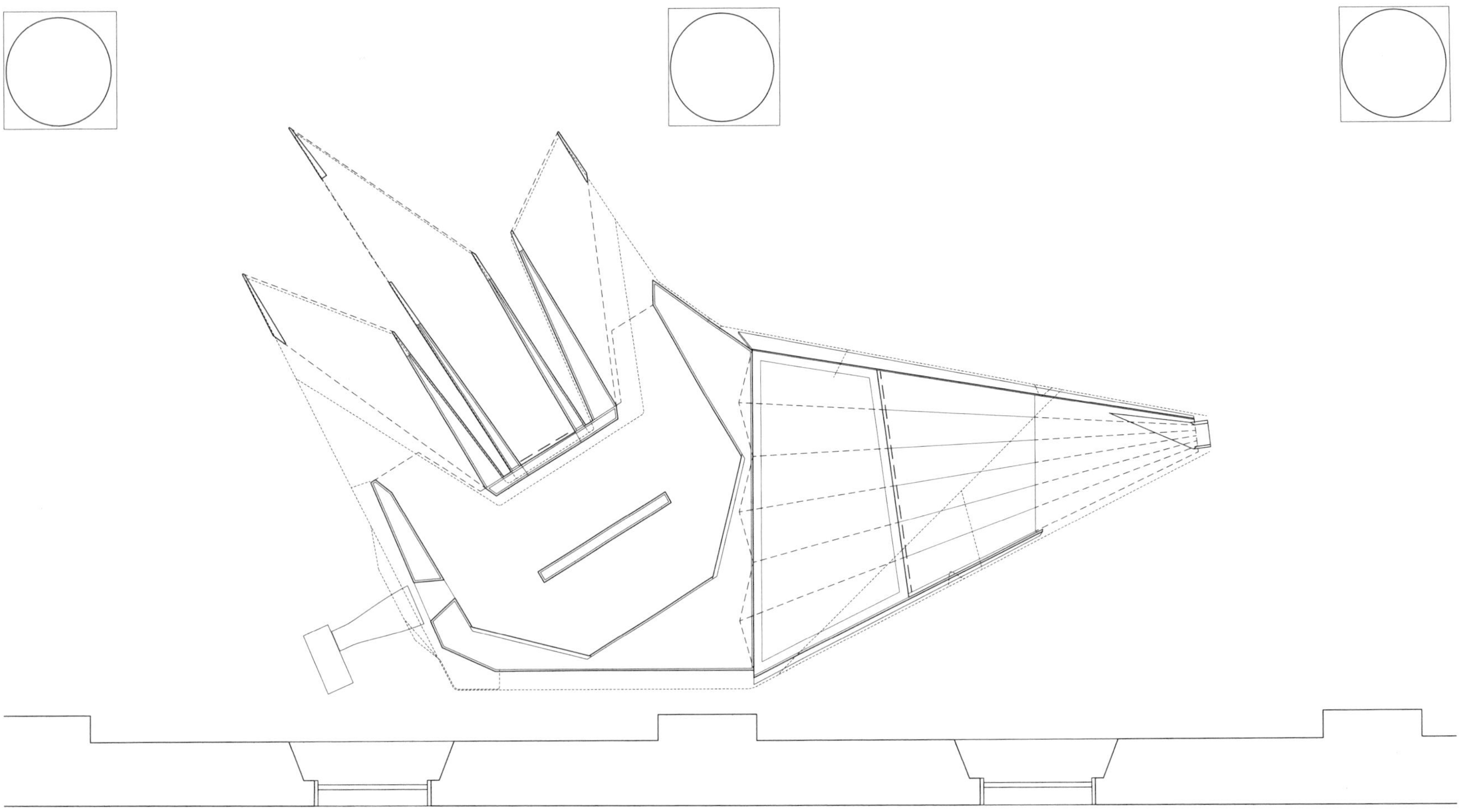

ACKNOWLEDGEMENTS

John Wardle Architects

    Design and Production Team
        John Wardle
        James Loder
        Alan Ting
        Stefan Mee
        Minnie Cade
        Alex Peck
        Andy Wong

    Initial Discussion Group
        Meaghan Dwyer
        Mathew van Kooy
        Adrian Bonaventura
        Adam Kolsrud
        Maya Borjesson
        Daniel Sykes
        Ariani Anwar
        Nick Roberts
        Rick Jordan
        Justine Makin

Artist

    Natasha Johns-Messenger

Film makers

    Coco and Maximilian

Fabrication

    Jacaranda Industries

Steelmaker

    Derek John

Structural Engineers

    Tensys

Glass Production

    Glass production management:
    Venice Art Factory Luca Berta e
    Francesca Giubilei

Photography

    Trevor Mein – Final Installation
    Adrian Bonaventura – Construction
    Process

Publication

    Uro Publications

Book Design

    Stuart Geddes

150

COLOPHON

First Published in 2018
by Uro Publications
Melbourne, Australia
uropublications.com

ISBN: 978-0-9943966-3-1

Full details of the Cataloguing-in-
Publication entry are available from the
National Library of Australia.

Sub-Editor Amelia Willis
Designed and typeset by Stuart Geddes
Printed and bound in The Netherlands
by Wilco Art Books